Revelation

Tanya G. Guleria

pencil

ISBN 978-93-5610-685-7
© Tanya G. Guleria 2022
Published in India 2022 by Pencil

A brand of

One Point Six Technologies Pvt. Ltd.
123, Building J2, Shram Seva Premises,
Wadala Truck Terminal, Wadala (E)
Mumbai 400037, Maharashtra, INDIA
E connect@thepencilapp.com
W www.thepencilapp.com

Author biography

Tanya G. Guleria is a bulgarian poet who lives and works in Germany. She has graduated medicine in the University of Varna. She is the author of several books with poetry and fables. As a follower of Aesopus and La Fontain she charms with her style and melodical expression sharing pieces of wisdom with her readers.

CONTENTS

Rag Doll

I am just a doll of ragsAnd I am torn and sewn -For future children just a bagAnd needless parts are pruned.The firstborn sin I am still rubbingFrom my forehead off -In land of men I'm meant for stubbing,Cause men are from above.I hide my freedom and my beautyUnder veils and headkerchiefs -Virtue is my real duty -Men are virtue thieves.Vanity is kept awayFrom my shallow mind -All I do is to obeyAlways low and kind.My husband is a god on Earth -He can beat and kill.There is no chance for new rebirth,Cause this is Allah's will.And this rag doll could not complain,Cause she lives perfect well.If death is all that has remained -She has a place in hell.

The Traitor

I am not sorry -I left you in the mud -You were only body, covered all with blood.My own survival -Was the highest goal -I had read the Bible, But not sure of all.Some call it a betrayal:All I want is life:To see again the rainbow:For that I'm going to strive.War is not my duty:Even with an oath:Death is not a beauty:To get it I'm too loath.

Winter Story

In the blizzard there was a sleighWhich was heading to its way.It had lost its safety trackAll around was cold and black.The human maintained its speedBy whipping hard the doggy breedCause in the storm he froze in fearHe hoped his saviours are near.But all the dogs pulled asideCause from the whip they tried to hide.The human from exhaustion droppedAnd the cruel whipping stopped.Dogs and man slept in the stormBack by back to keep them warm.Till the morning they survivedAll of them were still alive.Sometimes it is a wise decisionTo avoid all division.

Icarus

I've got wings and I am flying To the halo of the sun. In a minute I may be dying And all my dreams may be gone. But at least for one moment I am feeling I am free. But at least for this moment I will live, I will be.

Is it...

How much costs humiliation?Is someone willing to pay?Is it help, or a senseless donationthat would keep me alive for a day?Am I second quality person?Is it you that have to decide?Do I have to pray for some mercyOr my tears only to hide?Cause I know after so many lossesonly God knows what I have to winJust a die which destiny tossesHurting me is still your sin.

Comparison Steals Joy

Can you compare the wavesOf the almighty ocean?Maybe each one of you cravesPassion and truthful devotion.Aims depend on the ambition,Real is only endeavor.If you search for recognition,Search for it proper and clever!Over is always right.Never question God's power!Spend on your efforts some spite,Take criticism even sour!Earn approval for your work,Although it is always relative.Lie is good and truth is jerk,So success is comparative

Just remember my advice: Only pleased with yourselfYou will earn life's real prize.

Revolution

You lied to me -I'm going to hate you all I canAnd this will beMy revolution in a frying pan.

The Song of The Golden Prince (By Oscar Wilde)

The frowning time is passing on And burns away like fuel. My broken heart has turned to stone,My eyes are only jewel. And there is no persistent hope Left in the shop for buying. The only goods are hooks and rope -For safety or dying. Relax, not everything is lost -It's only phantom pain. I don't exist and real ghost Is never wet in rain.

Interview with God

Is there any value in my lifeYou asked me with some pain in your voice:- A lot of creatures have to strive,But staying on the Earth is your choice.- Will I find the meaning in existence,or the meaning will find me?- Lead your life with some resistanceAnd on your own you'll see.Cause value of the life know only theseWho created oneYour path is seldom blessed with easeIn case you track it you have won.

Vision

Change is what stops the life's switcherIt's equal for the poorest and the richer.Everyone will find the way,Cause it's not about feast and pray.Change is allembracing – body, soulIt brings one to the highest goal.It erases cruelty and shame,Cause things would never be again the same.You will not hear noise and crying.Cause everyone is somehow dying.You are entering the heaven's lifeAnd all you need would be so rife.Paradise is in your mindIf you search for it, then you will findBut do not wait for any new rebirthCause all you do comes back to EarthChange is not in the mightiest deathIt is in all the nature's breaths.If God is hidden inside youThe devil has nothing to do.

Cold

By the fireplace of personal wellbeingWe are sitting and champing some chips.We are watching around, but not seeing -All we do is giving good tips.And the cold outside is unreal, Someone's dying there - it is not us -We are speaking of bargain and deal,And are passing by them like a bus.And engulfed into sweetness and sleep, Real warmth is only outside.Cold possesses us into our deep, When for others we no warmth provide.

Sleep Well You Little Kids

In the clutches of uncertain world,With tears shedding from your lids,In ages humans bow to gold,Sleep well you little kids!Perhaps you didn't reach the coast,Or your house turned into tomb,Chased and hurt, killed or lost,Sleep calm in Gaya's womb!And if you play here for a while,Give joy with love so sheer,Sometimes the world deserves your smile,But not deserve your fear.

Importance

If the ocean exists on the Earth,It is full with the violence of life.Does it care who is killed, who is hurt,would it help if you crave to survive?If the Earth is giving us food,It also feeds its beasts of rapture.And if you are alone in the woods,No one knows who would be captured.And if you suffer a disease,And pray to God for some assistance - Perhaps God wishes to releasethe world from your poor existence.Life is great, but keep in mindThe meaning of this narrative:Be honest, good and kind,Cause your importance is comparative!

If

If God was like the way religions sayObsessed with the human betrayals,I would abandon all my faith awayThe way I abandoned my prayers.I can't imagine what it is beyondI am just afraid to disappear:Even not possessing all my flesh and bones,To my beloved I would be near.

Interesting Times

We live in interesting times
Sitting on the back seat.
The world is full with awful crimes
And everybody tries to cheat.

The press is pouring us with news,
Which damp our sanguinity.
Good is always going to lose -
Bad is handling all infinity.

In our hearts they feed our fear,
And it is growing like a beast:
How hope is going to appear
If we follow untrue priest?

"Divide and reign!", is their mark,
With which they rule our Earth -
A pack of wolfs and nasty sharks,
That only eat and hurt.

The tyrans sucking our blood,
Defending wealthy pockets:
They leave us drowning into mud,
Selling guns and rockets.

And we are waiting for some justice -
In life or after death,
But heaven comes when all in dust is,
And always waits ahead.

Why people lack belief in goodness?
Why do not dare to forgive?
Why we are treating al with rudeness?
And forget our lives to live?
I do not teach you to humanity,
But don't believe in lies.
Cause it would be insanity:
To hate, to kill, to die.

Oh, My God!

Sometimes misfortune comes to us,
Like heavy rain without shelter.
Evaporates all faith and trust,
As steel is liquified in melter.

And we are praying for some mercy,
Because it's hope, that dies at last.
And we are emptying our purses,
To make that God forgives our past.

But who is God? - Is he creator? -
The ruler of all universe?:
Or is he just a cruel traitor,
That threatens us with evil curse?

God is the one, who gives you bread,
When you are starving for some food -
He is the one, who lifts your head,
when you are feeling not so good.

And when you're lost, and when it hurts,
And your heart cries and howls -
There are a lot of gods on Earth,
Because God lives in all good souls.

Wise Thoughts

Stay calm when someone tries to lay
His foot on your way.
Anger is an awful vice
On which your enemy relies.

God knows better than the man in life
From what he craves for to deprive -
It would be for his destiny a crime,
If it comes, but in the unrightful time.

Choose frequently complicated ways,
And leave your competition in a maze -
It may be fatal if your right decision
Is taken with no time precision.

The Game

Life is like a game with dice:
Chance is giving you the aim,
But how your bet would rise
Depends on how you play the game.

It is only superstition:
Faith and hate, divide and reign.
Religion causes all partition -
It is a remedy for the insane.

Love is not our religion.
Love is our way of life.
The future shows only previsions,
For which we ought to strive.

The Dream

The world is sitting on a boiling pot
And every moment it is going to burst
Cause enemies are waiting for a shot
But no-one wants to shoot at first.

Cause politics has some protective rules
And one should break them with precision
Breaking is a matter of schedule
Of a non-suspectable prevision.

Create a problem to a blind society,
And pour them with some strong aggression.
Social behaviour loses variety
When put under the media pressure.

And lots of people screaming: "WAR!",
Proclaiming it as only way,
Cause politics is just a whore -
It works for those who pay.

So death is coming fast as train
To those who do not care,
Cause everybody is insane
And needs the greatest share.

The Wall

If all we have is walls
To keep us safe,
We just dig up the holes
Of our graves.

When borders grow as shrines
In our world -
Money is divine -
It is hope, that it is sold.

If we invest in guns -
Not in our kids -
Future is all done -
We are all in shits.

Wisdom

There is no wisdom in any war -
War is caused by vanity -
It leaves on Earth a nasty scar -
It is a real insanity.

Wisdom is avoiding trouble -
Tolerating the exceptions -
It is like a constant struggle -
With your own perceptions.

It is a law from above -
No wisdom has the one, who shoots -
And praising wisdom without love -
Is tearing flower from its roots.

Love, Hatred, Hope

Like the colours of the light
There are a lot of kinds of love.
It has an overwhelming might
As it is sent from God above.

Like the darkness of a pit
Hatred has no variations.
Hatred is the greatest cheat
Of the whole civilization.

Like the dawn after the night
Hope is rising in our mind,
Hope is giving us a sight,
That kindness is to give and find.

Once a Soul Asked an Angel

Once a soul asked an angel:
- Why should I go to Earth?
I am afraid of all the dangers,
That happen after birth.

The angel answered with warm voice:
- No reason for your fear,
Cause everytime you take a choice,
l will be always near.

- But how could I know you if
You change your face with other?
- For your ease and relief
You should call me mother.

Hatred

Hatred is too difficult to swallow:
That's why we spit it out all the time:
For people with a mind, which is too hollow:
Hatred leads them to the path of crime.

Sometimes it is politically propagated,
Based on past historical events:
Hatred is over and over created:
And for justice it always pretends.

Hatred is the root of all the evil:
Which is following us after birth -
Hatred rudimental, medieval:
Is still existing on the modern Earth.

The memory of hatred is outstanding:
Unfortunately more than we expect:
Hatred is always demanding:
And its demands is hard just to neglect.

Hatred is too difficult to swallow,
But do not spit it out too much,
Because it causes all the sorrow:
For those who get with it in touch.

Faith

Long ago was born a child -
It was gifted with such beauty -
That in the world so cruel and wild:
To defend it was a duty.

Its name was Faith and it was naked:
And people could not stand this fact:
They covered it with promise faked:
And forced it for the Might to act.

But Might was different in different regions:
And people built diverse shrines:
So in the world were born religions:
Which pretend to be divine.

And If you still remember Faith:
And ask what happened with its beauty?
- God knows how beauty to create:
Protecting it is our duty.

Beauty

This woman is of different breed
Not only seldom beauty.
Men are watching her with greed
Forgetting their duties.

She walks like floating in the air
Not stepping on the earth
And all her rivals only dare
Is pouring speech with dirt.

She is amazing even fallen
Her eyes are real universe.
And every word on earth is hollow
To describe such curse.

Cause beauty is a double dagger
And if you are too vain
You could sometimes stagger
And fall down in pain.

The Earth Is A Plate

The Earth is an enormous plate
Of which all people eat.
But if you open certain gate,
With serving or with cheat,
You get such kind of appetite,
That you're consuming all.
And with eager and with spite,
You mean that Earth's too small.

And you don't care about the others,
Cause they are just a competition,
And you don't have no friends and brothers -
Only partners with ambition
To gain much more than anyone.
It costs them too much nerve.
It costs a lot of blood and bones
To those, who don't deserve.

The Earth is an enormous plate
And to consume is fashion.
An evil malnutrition state,
Cause people lack compassion.

Who

What would you wish, when there is nothing more to lose?
When all your dreams are like a lotto game
You are the one who ought to choose
Who'll live, who'll die and who is now to blame.

What would you do if God is just a word
With which we calm our souls in front of death
Who will decide to cut the living cord
And who will stay alive instead?

Who has to live and who is just a bag
With guts and tissues and some blood
Our destiny we should until the end just drag
Cause we are made from spirit, faith and mud.

Forgive Us, Children,

Forgive us, children, for devastation,
for crimes, for wars because of greed.
Cause God gives life as a donation,
But it is power that we need.

And now the sky has turned to steel
And shoots with rockets on our hope,
Cause someone's made a nasty deal
And washes hands with human soap.

Life is worth less than a penny
Providing meat for Satan's feast
In the beginning of new Millennium
Man to man is still a beast.

Forgive us, but hunting for might
It is our souls that we sell.
And our hearts engulfed of spite
Deserve a place only in hell.

Because Most People Run Away

You do not prove intelligence
By the way you fight.
You just prove some diligence
To die for those in might.

Politicians fill their pockets,
Serving to the traders,
Which are selling guns and rockets
To invaded and invaders.

Journalists paint black and white
The "angels" and the "sinners".
Filling enemies with spite,
For those who pay the dinners.

Just listen to your life instinct
And drop the fucking gun today!
Humanity is not extinct
Because most people run away.

Immortality

When God created universe He made our choice reality:Multiplication is a curse,connected to mortality. The world blinked with its baby eyes -It had no brain to choose:It found that mother's love is nice, And chose its life to lose. And every time when you feel love, You make your choice ahead:To be eternal like a dove, Who dies to cheat the death.